BERND SCH

EGYPTIAN METALWORKING AND TOOLS

SHIRE EGYPTOLOGY

2

British Library Cataloguing in Publication Data:
Scheel, Bernd.
Egyptian metalworking and tools.
1. Egypt. Metalworking, ancient period.
I. Title.
684'.09'0932.
ISBN 0-7478-0001-4.

Published by
SHIRE PUBLICATIONS LTD,
Cromwell House, Church Street, Princes Risborough,
Aylesbury, Bucks HP17 9AJ, UK.

Series Editor: Barbara Adams.

ISBN 0 7478 0001 4

First published 1989.

Printed in Great Britain by
C. I. Thomas & Sons (Haverfordwest) Ltd,
Press Buildings, Merlins Bridge, Haverfordwest, Dyfed SA61 1XF.

Contents

LIST OF ILLUSTRATIONS 4
CHRONOLOGY 5
1. INTRODUCTION 7
2. MINING AND SMELTING 11
3. MELTING, CASTING AND PLATE PRODUCTION 21
4. FUNERARY EQUIPMENT AND OTHER ITEMS 34
5. TOOLS AND THEIR USES 47
6. THE SOCIAL STATUS AND ORGANISATION OF METALWORKERS 59
7. GLOSSARY 61
8. MUSEUMS 62
9. FURTHER READING 64
INDEX 67

Acknowledgements

I would like to thank Mrs Barbara Adams, Editor of the Shire Egyptology series, and Mr John Rotheroe of Shire Publications for their help, and my teacher, Professor Dr Hartwig Altenmuller of Hamburg University, for aiding investigations into Egyptian craftsmanship. I would also like to thank Professor Dr Rainer Stadelmann of the German Institute of Archaeology in Cairo for allowing me to publish new material from the metalworking site at the temple of King Seti I at Thebes. Mr Günter Heindl and Mrs Nicole Alexanian of the University of Heidelberg helped to evaluate the excavation results and Mrs Katharina Neumann of Frankfurt University analysed the excavated charcoal. Acknowledgement is made to Dr Rosemarie Drenkhahn of Kestner-Museum, Hanover; Dr Renate Germer of Hamburg University and Albrecht Germer; Professor Dr Silvio Curto of the Egyptian Museum, Turin; Dr Sylvia Schoske of the Staatliche Sammlung Ägyptischer Kunst in Munich; and Dr Joachim S. Karig of Ägyptisches Museum, Berlin SMPK, who provided photographs and permission for publication; other photographs and drawings are by the author. Finally, I would like to express my gratitude to my very understanding wife, Ursel, for all her support and help in my work. The outline dynastic chronology is based on that of Dr William J. Murnane and acknowledgement is made to him and Penguin Books for its use here.

List of illustrations

1. Map of early settlement and metallurgical sites *page 6*
2. Melters and a smith in a Fourth Dynasty Giza mastaba *page 9*
3. Map of ancient Egyptian mining districts *page 10*
4. Map showing a gold-bearing region in the eastern desert of Egypt *page 12*
5. Delivery of gold to temple and palace treasuries *page 13*
6. Goldworkers at work *page 13*
7. Isis kneeling on the hieroglyphic sign for gold *page 15*
8. Bowl furnace *page 16*
9. Shaft furnace *page 16*
10. Ritual of the 'opening of the mouth' *page 18*
11. Transport of copper, lead and tin *page 19*
12. Weighing of gold in the shape of rings *page 22*
13. Melting of metal, tomb of Mereruka *page 22*
14. Melting of metal, tomb of Pepiankh *page 23*
15. Egyptian melter with blowpipe *page 24*
16. Melting of metal, tomb of Puyemre *page 24*
17. Melter's dish bellows *page 25*
18. Melting and casting metal, tomb of Rekhmire *page 25*
19. Ancient metalworking site at funerary temple of King Seti I, Thebes *page 26*
20. Excavated hearths of foundry at the funerary temple of Seti I *page 26*
21. Hearth for metal melting *page 27*
22. Tuyères or clay nozzles from bellows *page 28*
23. Hearth with small casting mould *page 29*
24. Casting mould *page 29*
25. Pouring out molten metal, tomb of Pepiankh *page 30*
26. Pouring out molten metal, tomb of Mereruka *page 30*
27. Metalworkers' workshop: melting, casting and hammering out of metal *page 31*
28. Tools of a blacksmith or metalbeater *page 31*
29. Blacksmith or metalbeater at work *page 31*
30. Annealing a metal object *page 31*
31. Smith at a brazier *page 32*
32. Annealing in a fireplace fanned by dish bellows *page 32*
33. Gold beater's tools *page 33*
34. Production of a libation vessel *page 35*
35. Hand-basin and ewer set *page 35*
36. Production of a hand-basin *page 36*
37. Smith working at a wooden anvil *page 36*
38. Bronze flask and ring stand *page 37*
39. Polishing an offering stand *page 37*
40. Bronze censer handle *page 38*
41. Seti I censing and libating in front of Sokar *page 38*
42. Vessel polishing *page 39*
43. Outline drawer and engraver at work *page 39*
44. Engraver at work *page 39*
45. Statuette of the crocodile god Sobek *page 41*
46. Mirror with handle in shape of nude woman *page 42*
47. Statuette of Isis with Horus on her lap *page 43*
48. Bronze ram's head finial *page 43*
49. Drilling of precious stones *page 45*
50. Manufacture of a collar *page 45*
51. Different types of axe-blade *page 48*
52. Woodcutter, tomb of Nefer and Kahay *page 48*
53. Different types of adze-blade *page 49*
54. Carpenter working with an adze *page 50*
55. Carpenter working with a saw *page 51*
56. Carpenters cutting out ornaments *page 51*
57. Wood sculptors at work *page 52*
58. Drilling wood and stone *page 52*
59. Manufacture of sandals and leather straps *page 54*
60. Box with medical instruments *page 55*
61. Razor and hair-curler *page 57*
62. Map of ancient Egypt *page 66*

Chronology

Predynastic	5500 - 3050 BC	
	5500 - 4000	
	Lower Egypt	Fayum A. Merimda
	Upper Egypt	Badarian
	4000 - 3500	
	Lower Egypt	?Omari A
	Upper Egypt	Amratian (Naqada I)
	3500 - 3300	
	Lower Egypt	?Omari B
	Upper Egypt	Early Gerzean (Naqada II)
	3500 - 3050	
	Lower Egypt	Maadi
	3300 - 3150	
	Upper Egypt	Late Gerzean (Naqada II)
Protodynastic	3200 - 3050 BC	Naqada III (Late Gerzean)
Early Dynastic	3050 - 2613 BC	Dynasties I - II
Old Kingdom	2613 - 2181 BC	Dynasties III - VI
First Intermediate Period	2181 - 2040 BC	Dynasties VII - XI(1)
Middle Kingdom	2040 - 1782 BC	Dynasties XI(2) - XII
Second Intermediate Period	1782 - 1570 BC	Dynasties XIII - XVII
New Kingdom	1570 - 1070 BC	Dynasties XVIII - XX
Third Intermediate Period	1070 - 713 BC	Dynasties XXI - XXIV
Late Period	713 - 332 BC	Dynasties XXV - XXXI
Graeco-Roman Period	332 BC - AD 395	Ptolemies and Roman Emperors

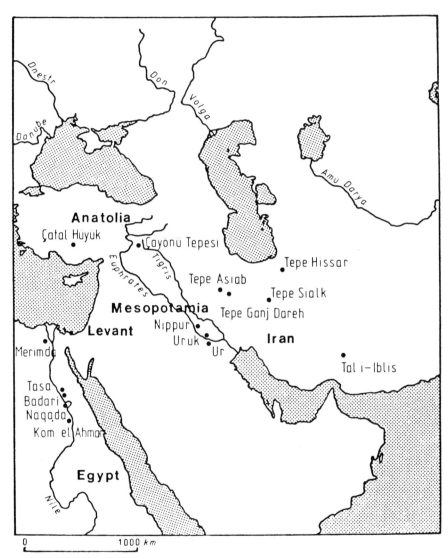

1. Early settlement and metallurgical sites in the Near East.

1
Introduction

The development of metallurgy

The exact chronology and geography of the earliest practice of metallurgy are still matters for discussion between archaeologists and technologists. The early centres of mining and metal processing can be identified (figure 1) but details of their growth and their influence on other regions remain unknown.

The development of trades and crafts is closely connected with social evolution: with the process of settlement, the transition from food-collecting to food-producing economies and the domestication of animals and plants. These changes made possible production of surplus food for those who were specially talented at crafts or metalworking.

In the Near East, the process of settlement may have begun as early as 10,000 BC. In the ninth and eighth millennia BC farming communities arose at Tepe Ganj Dareh and Tepe Asiab in the Zagros Mountains in south-western Iran. Early farming communities were also founded in the Levant and in southern Anatolia.

The earliest indications of metallurgy in the Near East have been found in Anatolia and Iran. Native copper was used for the manufacture of jewellery in Anatolia as early as 6500 BC: Çayönü Tepesi and Çatal Hüyük are well known sites where pieces of metalwork have been found. Smelted copper has been found in those areas as well as in Iran. The early metallurgical sites in Iran are Tepe Sialk, where the metal artefacts date to approximately 5500 to 5000 BC; Tal i-Iblis, with artefacts from about 5000 to 4500 BC; and Tepe Hissar, with metalwork of about 3500 BC.

Ideal conditions for the process of settlement and the development of farming were found in the major river valleys of western Asia. Extensive irrigation systems there made possible the production of enough food to support not only the agriculturalists but also non-food-producing specialists like craftsmen, priests, artists and administrators. The growth of the early urban civilisations in the Nile valley, the Tigris-Euphrates valley and the Indus valley was characterised by intensive food production, technological and industrial development (including metal processing) and external trade, as well as the invention of writing. The earliest of these three civilisations was the Sumerian, in the Tigris-Euphrates valley of Mesopotamia where extensive cities like Ur, Uruk and Nippur arose in the course of the fourth millennium BC. The craftsmen, especially the Sumerian smiths, showed remarkable skills. As well as neolithic techniques like hammering, bending, cutting, grinding and polishing, the Sumerian smiths mastered annealing, smelting, melting and casting metals. It is possible that the early technological developments in Mesopotamia took place under the influence of Anatolian and Iranian immigrants: the Tigris and the Euphrates rise in Anatolia and very early Iranian settlements in the Zagros Mountains border the area east of Mesopotamia. There is, however, no firm archaeological evidence for this belief. Nevertheless, trade in raw materials or metal products and contacts with itinerant smiths from Anatolia and Iran could have been the decisive factor in the independent development of a Mesopotamian metal-processing industry.

Early Egypt

Evolutionary stages similar to those seen in Mesopotamia may be observed in early Egypt. Archaeological research in the Nile valley indicates that the process of neolithic settlement took place in the course of the sixth millennium BC, as demonstrated by artefacts, bones and different kinds of grain found during excavations at the sites of Merimda in the south-west Delta, Tasa in Upper Egypt and those in the Fayum basin. Another well known neolithic settlement is Badari, which is south of modern Asyut in Middle Egypt. Although excavations at Badari revealed the very first Egyptian metal artefacts, metalworking was not common in this phase of neolithic Egypt and the metal objects found at Badari have to be recognised as isolated occurrences of copper beads used as burial objects.

Metal processing became more common during the chalcolithic Naqada I-III cultures (named after the Upper Egyptian site at which they were first identified and classified into relatively dated phases of settlement from about 4000 to 3000 BC). Naqada is situated about 27 km (17 miles) north of modern Luxor. The Naqada I culture (*c*. 4000-3500 BC) exhibits a well developed pottery manufacture and also a stone vase industry in which metal tools were used, but no evidence of metal production has been discovered. In the following Naqada II and III phases (about 3500 to 3050 BC) foreign influence caused a turning point in the development of early Egypt. The Naqada II culture spread over the entire Nile valley from north of Hierakonpolis into the Delta. Long-distance trade and possibly contact with immigrants brought new technologies and materials into Predynastic Egypt. Pottery

2. Melters with blowpipes work around a charcoal fireplace; a smith hammers out a plate. (After Dunham and Simpson, *Giza Mastabas I, The Mastaba of Queen Meresankh III*, Boston, 1974, figure 5.)

and stone vessels were imported from Mesopotamia and it is reasonable to suppose that the growth of Predynastic Egyptian metallurgy was influenced by Mesopotamian technologies as metal processing had a longer tradition in the Tigris-Euphrates valley.

However, little is known about the techniques applied, the manufacturing processes used and the working conditions of the early metalworkers in the Nile valley. Our knowledge of metallurgy in this early period is based on the scientific analysis of artefacts, which indicates that copper casting was practised as early as the late Naqada II and Naqada III periods of about 3300 to 3000 BC. Copper tools and weapons were manufactured simply by open-mould casting. Melting, casting and smelting metals from ores required a sophisticated pottery industry, which would then have served as a basis for acquiring the technique of producing high temperatures using charcoal and developing smelting furnaces and melting crucibles.

From the beginning of the Dynastic Period in Egypt in about 3050 BC metal-processing techniques were continuously developed and refined. With the centralisation of the Egyptian administration and the formation of a cultural centre at the royal capital, various professions and trades were established. Although Egypt was neither the earliest nor the most important metallurgy centre at that time, the first pictorial and inscriptional sources relating to the metalworker's craft come from Egyptian mastaba tombs at the beginning of the Old Kingdom. The first scenes of metalworking were found in Giza on the walls of the tomb of Queen

Meresankh III, the wife of King Khaefre (figure 2). Similar depictions of metalworkers and their craft are found in the tombs of officials in all periods of Egyptian history. Pictorial, inscriptional and archaeological sources, including the metal artefacts themselves, together serve as the basis for our investigation into Egyptian metalworking.

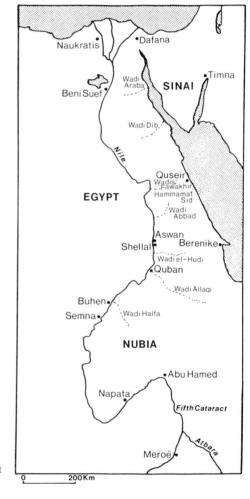

3. Distribution map of ancient Egyptian mining districts.

2
Mining and smelting

In ancient Egypt metals were mined in several areas, by open-cast as well as by underground mining (figure 3). Gold and copper were the first ones processed by the early Egyptian metalworkers. Later in the development of Egyptian metallurgy, electrum, silver, iron, tin, bronze, lead and platinum were also worked. In addition, traces of nickel, zinc, arsenic, antimony and cobalt have been detected in small amounts in metal artefacts. Metals were also imported by trade or as a tribute from neighbouring countries, especially gold and copper, of which great quantities were used.

Gold
Native gold was processed into small items of jewellery as early as the Predynastic Period. During the Old Kingdom Egyptian miners, supported by the local nomadic population, started mining for gold in the eastern desert. Ancient Egyptian records provide details of the principal mines. The 'Gold of the Desert from Koptos' was mined at several sites near Wadi Hammamat, Wadi Abbed, Wadi el-Fawakhir and Wadi Sid. An ancient Egyptian sketch map of this area exists, showing the gold-mining district. The hieratic captions describe the location of a gold mine, with paths leading to the Red Sea, the miners' quarters, the gold-bearing mountain areas and gold-washing stations (figure 4). This sketch map, drawn on a papyrus, dates from the New Kingdom and is regarded as the first map in history.

From the beginning of the Middle Kingdom the gold deposits of northern Nubia were exploited. Egyptian records tell of the 'Gold of Wawat', which was mined near Wadi Allaqi, Wadi el-Hudi and between Buhen and Semna. The Egyptian influence on Nubia developed quickly during the New Kingdom and another gold-mining district was opened up south of the gold mines of Wawat. Egyptian records mention the 'Gold of Kush' which was mined in the area of Napata and Abu Hamed. In Egypt, the pure metal was extracted both from alluvial gold found in surface deposits and from sub-surface quartz gold.

There are no ancient Egyptian descriptions of the way in which the pure metal was extracted from the quartz ores, but a report written by the Greek traveller Agatharchides of Cnidus, who lived in the second century BC, describes the working conditions

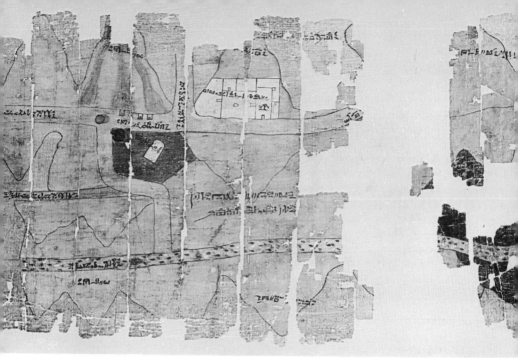

4. The first map in history, showing a gold-mining district. (Museo Egizio, Turin, 1879, 1899, 1969.)

and techniques applied in an Egyptian gold mine of the Ptolemaic Period. From Agatharchides' observations it seems that many workers, commanded by overseers, had to work very hard under painful conditions. Criminals and prisoners of war were condemned to the gold mines, as well as unjustly accused innocent people, because there was a great demand for profit-making cheap labour. The captives were bound in chains and had no chance of escape from the desert mining district. The guards were made up of foreign soldiers who could not understand the language of the captured workers, so no one was able to make friendly contact with his keepers or to corrupt the soldiers. The captives had to work day and night, without respite.

As this report dates from the Ptolemaic Period there is no evidence that working conditions were the same in the earlier periods of Pharaonic Egypt. However, with regard to Agatharchides' account of the methods of extraction employed, there would have been no major changes from the processes of gold-mining developed earlier in Egyptian history. Agatharchides says that the gold-bearing rock face was first burnt to crumble it. Then the strongest workers broke the quartz rock with hammers. In this way tunnels and shafts were cut through the mine. Inside the dark passages the captives had to carry oil lamps bound on their foreheads. The cut blocks were thrown on the ground

5. The delivery of gold in the form of rings, small bags of gold dust and ingots to temple and palace treasuries. (After Davies, *The Tomb of Rekh-Mi-Re at Thebes*, New York, 1943, plates 18, 19.)

behind the miners and young boys then had to gather up the blocks to take them out into the open. Outside the entrance workers over thirty years of age crushed the gold-bearing blocks in mortars into small pieces the size of a pea. Women and older men ground the small pieces to powder with grinding mills. (Mills for grinding quartz ore have been found in Wadi el-Hudi and Wadi Hammamat.) After grinding the pulverised quartz was washed on a sloping surface where the heavy gold dust remained

6. Goldworkers producing precious objects for daily use and funerary equipment. (After Davies, *The Tomb of Two Sculptors at Thebes*, New York, 1925, plate 11.)

while the other matter, the gangue, was washed away. As an enormous amount of water was needed, it seems likely that the gold-bearing siliceous dust was sometimes carried to the banks of the Nile for washing and then refining.

From the beginning of the Ptolemaic Period the gold dust was refined by melting it together with a special mixture of lead, tin, salt and barley bran, as is explained by Agathar-chides. The pure metal extracted was carried to the treasuries of the temples and palaces in the shape of rings, ingots, nuggets or small bags of gold dust (figure 5). The treasury administrators supplied the precious metal to metalworkers, goldsmiths and jewellers who manufactured gold objects for daily use as well as for ritual purposes and funerary equipment (figure 6).

Gods, goddesses and the king himself had special relationships with gold. The sun god Re was honoured as 'Gold of Stars'. Horus was called 'Child of Gold' or 'Falcon of Gold' and the king, as the personification of Horus or the falcon on earth, was named 'Mountain of Gold'. Isis, the mother of Horus, and her sister, Nephthys, are often shown on royal sarcophagi from the New Kingdom: kneeling or standing on the hieroglyphic sign for gold, they are protecting the deceased pharaoh (figure 7).

Copper

Copper was another very important metal. It was the most common metal for everyday use in ancient Egypt and was made into vessels, tools and weapons. Because of its natural content of arsenic, Egyptian copper was particularly hard. Copper ores like malachite, azurite, chrysocolla and copper pyrites were mined and smelted in the eastern desert and in Sinai. The invention or introduction of the smelting process also marked the beginning of the metal period in ancient Egypt because mass-production of metal objects became possible. In the eastern desert copper ores were exploited east of Beni Suef in the Wadi Araba, north-west of Berenike and east of Quban. In Sinai highly productive copper mines have been excavated at Timna near Eilat. Copper was also imported from Cyprus and the Near East. It is difficult to say exactly when copper began to be mined in Sinai and in the other mining districts but it is certain that mining was practised in Timna from the mid Eighteenth Dynasty.

After the mining district had been prospected by experienced mineralogists, the miners cut out the copper-bearing minerals. The crude ore was crushed into small pieces, milled and winnowed to separate the associated minerals from the metal-bearing ore.

7. The goddess Isis kneeling on the hieroglyphic sign for gold, depicted on a sarcophagus from the tomb of King Amenophis II in the Valley of the Kings.

The ground ore was smelted in furnaces of different kinds. The simplest and probably the oldest type was a primitive bowl furnace dug into the ground (figure 8). In the course of the smelting process a mixture of crushed malachite and charcoal, the charge, was roasted and reduced to small prills of rich copper ore embedded in a copper slag. The prills were extracted by crushing the slag and then melted together to form copper ingots.

In Ramesside times sophisticated shaft furnaces were used which enabled higher temperatures of about 1200 C (2200 F) to be reached (figure 9). The brick-built furnaces were loam-lined and fitted with a tap hole; the heat was intensified by blasts from bellows. In the course of the smelting process the copper droplets sank to the furnace bottom, forming an ingot. At the end of the process the lighter slag above the smelted metal could be tapped into a slag pit through the tap hole in the furnace wall. Afterwards the copper ingot was removed from the bottom of the furnace.

Electrum

Another metal known as early as the Predynastic Period was electrum, which was found as a native alloy of gold and silver. In early times it was used only for the manufacture of valuable

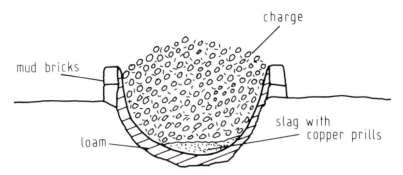

8. Early bowl furnace for primitive smelting.

9. Sophisticated shaft furnace for the smelting of metal from its ores.

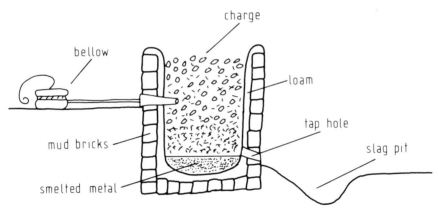

jewellery because of its rarity. Electrum was mainly imported from Nubia and the land of Punt and up to the New Kingdom it was also manufactured artificially by alloying gold and silver in appropriate proportions. Apart from the manufacture of jewellery, electrum was also used for the production of funerary equipment like vessels, statues, offering stands and the finger and toe sheaths of royal mummies. The walls and doors of temples were covered with electrum plates, as were the pyramidal tops of obelisks.

Silver

Although silver was also used in Egypt as early as the Naqada II period in Predynastic times, there is no evidence that the Egyptians themselves mined silver anywhere in the country. On the contrary, it has been proved from ancient Egyptian records that silver was imported from Mesopotamia, Crete and Cyprus. A lead-silver mine, worked from about 3000 BC, was discovered on Siphnos, an island of the Cyclades. Metalworkers used silver for the manufacture of jewellery, vessels, offering stands, coffins, sarcophagi, musical instruments, scarabs, statues, mirrors and other valuable items.

According to Agatharchides silver was extracted from crude gold by cementation or cupellation in the course of the gold-refining process. Silver was called 'white metal' by the Egyptians and it was believed that the bones of the gods were of silver and their flesh of gold.

Iron

Iron was another metal of mythical character. According to legend, the skeleton of Seth, the god of wind and storms, lord of the desert and enemy of Osiris and Horus, was of iron. Iron was called the 'metal of heaven' because for a long time the Egyptians knew only meteoric iron, which has a high nickel content. Because of its supposedly divine origin, meteoric iron was used in particular for the production of protective amulets and magic model tools which were needed for the ritual called the 'opening of the mouth', a ceremony which was necessary to prepare the mummy of the deceased for life after death (figure 10). In the Eighteenth Dynasty telluric iron was imported from the Peloponnese and from the Near East, especially from the Mitanni and Hittite Anatolia and probably from Cyprus. Egypt itself has some remarkable iron ore deposits, but there is no evidence that these deposits were ever worked before the Late or Graeco-Roman periods.

There is haematite in Sinai and in the Wadi Dib, while the Wadi Araba in the eastern desert contains ferruginous limestone. There is limonite in the Wadi Marwat and the Wadi Halfa contains banks of oolitic ironstone. Exhausted iron mines were discovered in the Wadi Hammamat, but there is no evidence that these were exploited in Pharaonic times. Egyptian magnetite deposits in the eastern desert between Aswan and Shellal were mined and smelted after the sixth century BC.

The earliest indications of iron smelting in Egypt were found in the Delta region. Excavations at the site of Naucratis and Defenna revealed a large quantity of iron slag and some ore. The site of Naucratis can be dated to about 580 BC. Iron tools manufactured from telluric iron appeared in 650 BC during the

10. The ritual of the 'opening of the mouth', from the tomb of Inherkhau (number 359) in Deir el-Medina, of the Nineteenth Dynasty. The ceremony is carried out by the hawk-god in front of the mummy of the deceased with the use of a ceremonial adze.

Saite Period. Excavations at Meroe, which is situated on the Nile in the Sudan about 200 km (125 miles) north-east of Khartoum, confirmed that iron smelting from pulverised haematite took place from the third century BC to the Roman Period.

Tin

The occurrence of tin in Egypt is a question much debated amongst archaeologists and technologists. Egyptian tin deposits exist in the eastern desert near Quseir el-Qadim and in Nubia near the Fifth Cataract, but there are no signs that the cassiterite deposits were ever mined in Dynastic Egypt. Tin had to be imported. Our present knowledge indicates that tin could have been imported by intermediate trade with Crete and Cyprus from Spain and Britain, especially from Devon and Cornwall. Mesopotamia probably obtained tin from south-east Asia: tin occurs in Malaysia, Indonesia and Thailand. Long-distance trade from such areas might have brought tin via the Indus civilisation to Egypt, though this trade cannot be proved. For a long time it was believed that tin was mined in the Caucasus, Iran and Anatolia and delivered to Egypt, but it is now known that there are no tin deposits in these areas. During the first century AD Egypt even took an intermediate part in the tin trade and exported tin to Somalia and India.

Tin was mainly used for the production of tin bronze, which was known by the Twelfth Dynasty. At that time there could have been no imports of pure tin reaching Egypt, but imports of already alloyed tin bronze came from Syria, where rich trading centres like Mari, Alalakh, Aleppo, Ras Shamra and Byblos flourished. The exact date when the Egyptians started their own tin bronze production is unknown, but Egyptian metalworkers probably began to alloy copper with tin early in the New Kingdom.

A scene from the tomb of the Vizier Rekhmire at Thebes shows the delivery of different kinds of metals needed for the casting of a bronze door for the temple of Karnak (figure 11). Hieroglyphic inscriptions report the 'bringing of Asiatic metal'. One man bears a big copper ox-hide ingot, while his two fellows

11. Three workers carry copper in the shape of an ox-hide ingot and baskets containing small rounded ingots of lead and tin. An overseer supervises the porters. (After Davies, *The Tomb of Rekh-Mi-Re at Thebes*, New York, 1943, plate 53.)

transport baskets filled with small ingots, probably of tin and lead. Tin bronze was used for the production of mirrors, vessels, tools, weapons and for the casting of statues.

Lead

In addition to copper and iron, lead was also smelted from its ores in Egypt. Galena was mined in the eastern desert at Quseir el-Qadim and certain other deposits near the Red Sea were exploited. Lead was known in Egypt as early as the Predynastic Period. Throughout Egyptian history galena was used as an eye-paint (kohl). Small figures, net sinkers and jewellery were manufactured in lead from the time of the Old Kingdom. In the New Kingdom there was an increasing need for lead, which was therefore imported from Syria and Cyprus. From about the end of the New Kingdom lead was commonly used for alloying leaded tin bronze. The addition of lead to bronze increases the fluidity of the alloy and lowers its melting point so that the casting of large or very detailed objects becomes easier.

All the metals described were used by Egyptian smiths or goldsmiths, who became increasingly important in society during the course of Egyptian civilisation.

3
Melting, casting and plate production

After the local or imported crude metal had been delivered to the storehouses of temples and palaces, it was weighed and registered by the Egyptian temple or palace administration. Before a quantity of metal was dispensed from the storehouses to the metalworkers for further processing, the metal had to be weighed again, to control the stock of metals and to prevent embezzlement. Storehouse officials are shown using a pair of scales while a scribe makes a note of the result (figure 12). The weighing scenes in Egyptian tombs often depict the posts of the balances crowned by the head of the goddess Maat, bearing an ostrich feather. Maat, the daughter of the sun god Re, was, among other things, a symbol of truth and justice; she ensured a correct and exact result in weighing.

The wall paintings, reliefs and hieroglyphic inscriptions in Egyptian private tombs do not always specify the kind of metal which is being worked by the smiths or metalworkers. However, several inscriptions do name the type of raw material or it can be identified by its colour or shape. The techniques of melting, casting and plate production, which are important basic requirements for further precise working, are comparable for the different metals.

Melting the metal

The first job which had to be done by the metalworkers in the temple or palace workshops was the melting of the crude metal. Egyptian pictorial and inscriptional sources depict the melting of copper, gold, silver, tin bronze or leaded tin bronze. In Old and Middle Kingdom times the melting of copper or arsenic copper for the production of vessels and tools for daily use was very common. In the course of the Middle Kingdom and in later periods tin bronze and leaded tin bronze were used. Silver and gold served throughout Egyptian history as the basic materials for objects of royal use or for funerary and temple equipment.

The metal had to be melted because large ingots or other shapes of crude metal, which were customary in the trade, had to be refined or alloyed for casting or split up into smaller portions for further treatment by the smiths. Melting is depicted in nearly every wall painting or relief showing Egyptian metalworking, so

12. The weighing of gold in the shape of rings. A scribe makes a note of the result while his colleague operates the balance. (After Davies, *The Tombs of Menkheperrasonb, Amenmose and Another*, London, 1933, plate 11.)

technological innovations from the Old Kingdom to the Ptolemaic Period can be traced by studying metalworking scenes and inscriptions in Egyptian tombs.

The metal was melted in one or more crucibles, depending on the amount required. In the Sixth Dynasty tomb of the Vizier Mereruka at Saqqara six metalworkers are depicted sitting around

13. A fireplace containing two crucibles side by side is fanned by six melters using blowpipes. As written in hieroglyphics, one of the melters right of the crucibles says to his workmates:D'It's a new crucible, come to its side, comrade'. Above the scene are shown finished metal vessels. (After Duell, *The Mastaba of Mereruka*, Chicago, 1938, plate 30.)

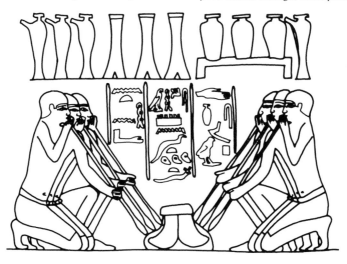

14. Three melters at work. The crucible leans against a low wall. The hieroglyphic inscription includes the order to blast air into the fireplace. (After Blackman, *The Rock-Tombs of Meir V*, London, 1953, plate 17.)

a hearth or fireplace containing two crucibles side by side. In the tomb of the Vizier Pepiankh at Meir, also of the Sixth Dynasty, only one crucible is shown, leaning against a low wall, probably built of mud bricks, with three metalworkers sitting in front of the hearth (figure 14).

The hearths were charcoal-fired; charcoal was burnt extensively in the eastern desert and the Sinai. Temperatures of about 1000 C (1800 F) or even more could be achieved if the embers of the charcoal fire were aroused with suitable tools. In earlier times fans of foliage might have been employed to provide a draught. In the Old and Middle Kingdoms Egyptian metalworkers or melters used blowpipes consisting of reeds with clay tips. With blowpipes a strong blast of air could be directed precisely on to the glowing charcoal below the bottom of the crucible (figure 15). There is evidence that Middle Kingdom metalworkers used skin bellows, as mentioned in a text written on a coffin, although skin bellows, probably manufactured from the skin of a goat or a gazelle, have not been found in Egyptian depictions.

Much more effective than fans, blowpipes or skin bellows were pot, drum or dish bellows. The earliest known depiction of dish bellows is in a melting scene on a relief inside the Eighteenth Dynasty tomb of the priest Puyemre, the Second Prophet of the

15. Egyptian melter with his blow-pipe.

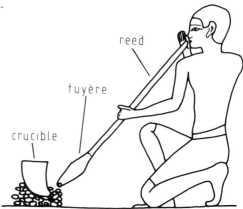

reed

tuyère

crucible

god Amun in Thebes (figure 16). In this scene a metalworker, with a blowpipe in his left hand and a stick in his right hand, supervises the melting process and prepares the molten metal for casting while his colleague operates a pair of dish bellows. The dishes were of pottery, wood or stone fitted with skin or leather coverings. A reed or pipe connected the dish of the bellows with clay nozzles or tuyères leading into the fire (figure 17). When the covering was pulled up the dish was filled with air; when it was pressed down air was blown through the reed and tuyères into the fireplace. The introduction of dish bellows was crucial to enable the large quantities of metal used for the casting of large metal objects to be melted, as shown on a wall painting in the tomb of the Vizier Rekhmire at Thebes. In that foundry four hearths fired by charcoal are fanned by several dish bellows to melt a large

16. Two metalworkers, using a dish bellows and blowpipe, are melting metal. (After Davies, *The Tomb of Puyemrê at Thebes I*, New York, 1922, plate 28.)

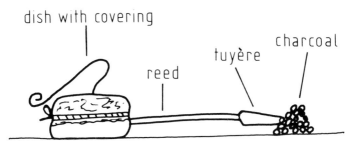

17. A typical dish bellows used by ancient Egyptian melters.

18. The melting and casting of metal. (After Davies, *The Tomb of Rekh-Mi-Re at Thebes*, New York, 1943, plate 52.)

quantity of metal, probably leaded tin bronze, for the casting of the leaves of a door intended for the Great Temple of Amun in Karnak (figure 18).

Although private tombs show many scenes of ancient foundries, no metalworking site of this kind had been unearthed in the Nile valley until, in the spring of 1985, Professor Dr Rainer Stadelmann of the German Institute of Archaeology in Cairo discovered an ancient Egyptian foundry at the funerary temple of King Seti I in the Theban necropolis (figure 19). The metalworking site can be dated by pottery to the Ptolemaic Period, a time when the funerary temple had already lost its function of maintaining the cult of the deceased king. Four mud-brick structures of different lengths, each built of two parallel brick settings, were excavated (figure 20). These served as hearths for the crucibles (figure 21); the smaller hearths were 1.4 metres (5 feet) in length and the two larger ones 7 metres (23 feet). A small hearth had room for one

19. Excavation of an ancient Egyptian foundry of the Ptolemaic Period at the funerary temple of Seti I at Thebes.

20. The excavated hearths of the foundry at the funerary temple of King Seti I.

21. One of the two smaller hearths from the metalworking site at the funerary temple of King Seti I at Thebes.

crucible, a larger one was built to hold about five crucibles.

It was possible, therefore, either to mass-produce many objects or to cast large ones at this site. For the melting process the gap between the low parallel brick constructions was filled with charcoal. Analysis of pieces of charcoal found *in situ* inside the hearths show that acacia wood was used to produce charcoal. In the Nile valley the plentiful acacia wood was in very common use for shipbuilding, as building timber and for the production of coffins, doors and chariots. The charcoal analysed contained *Acacia nilotica* and probably *Acacia raddiana* or *Acacia seyal*. The hearths held the blowing charcoal together under the crucibles. Many crucible sherds, broken tuyères and the nozzles of dish bellows were found at the site (figure 22).

Casting

A small limestone casting mould was found *in situ* beside one of the small hearths at the excavated site and another one was excavated unstratified (figures 23 and 24). These moulds were not used for producing objects by open-mould casting but to split the molten metal into smaller portions for further treatment by the smiths, who manufactured plates and sheet metal from the small

22. Some broken tuyères or clay nozzles from the metalworking site at the funerary temple of Seti I at Thebes.

portions. Moulds of this kind are shown on paintings and reliefs in private tombs as early as the Old Kingdom, as illustrated by a scene in the tomb of the Vizier Pepiankh at Meir, where a metalworker is pouring the molten metal into a mould (figure 25). To protect his hands, the worker used stones or blocks of wood to hold the very hot crucible. Sometimes, while the metal was being poured, another worker tried to hold back any contamination in the crucible (figure 26).

Plate production

After being melted, refined and divided into portions, the cooled metal was passed to the smiths or blacksmiths for plate or sheet production, as is shown in the Fifth Dynasty tomb of the boundary official Wepemnefret in Giza (figure 27). Egyptian blacksmiths used very simple tools. The metal was beaten on an anvil made of stone (probably of basalt, diorite or granite) which was placed on a wooden block to absorb the hammering. The metalworkers beat the plates with simple hammer stones without a shaft (figure 28). Two kinds of hammer stones were in use: one with a flat face and the other with a rounded one. A flat hammer stone was needed for smoothing the metal, while a rounded one was used for chasing. Smoothing and chasing hammer stones are

23. (Left) One of the smaller hearths with a casting mould found *in situ* at the metal-working site at the funerary temple of King Seti I at Thebes.

24. (Below) Casting mould excavated unstratified at the metal-working site at the funerary temple of King Seti I at Thebes.

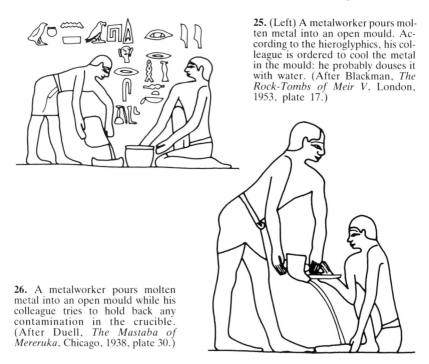

25. (Left) A metalworker pours molten metal into an open mould. According to the hieroglyphics, his colleague is ordered to cool the metal in the mould: he probably douses it with water. (After Blackman, *The Rock-Tombs of Meir V*, London, 1953, plate 17.)

26. A metalworker pours molten metal into an open mould while his colleague tries to hold back any contamination in the crucible. (After Duell, *The Mastaba of Mereruka*, Chicago, 1938, plate 30.)

depicted in private tombs from Old Kingdom times to the Ptolemaic Period. A wall painting from the tomb of the Vizier Rekhmire shows the process of chasing (figure 29). With his left hand a blacksmith holds a plate on an anvil while his right hand energetically beats the metal with the rounded chasing hammer stone.

Egyptian metalworkers had mastered the technique for annealing as early as the Predynastic Period. In the course of the chasing process the beaten piece of metal became hard and brittle and further treatment of the cold metal could cause it to crack. The piece had, therefore, to be heated or annealed, which caused a rearrangement of the crystalline structure of the metal and made it ductile again. While in the Old and Middle Kingdoms annealing took place in a fireplace on the floor of the workshop (figure 30), New Kingdom metalworkers made themselves much more comfortable. In the tomb of the Vizier Rekhmire a wall painting shows a smith sitting on a stool in front of a brazier (figure 31). To anneal his piece of metal he holds it with tongs in the glowing charcoal of the brazier. The fire is fanned by a blowpipe. If large

27. Four melters are melting metal; a worker is pouring the molten metal into a mould; two smiths are hammering out a plate. (After Hassan, *Excavations at Giza II*, Cairo, 1936, figure 219.)

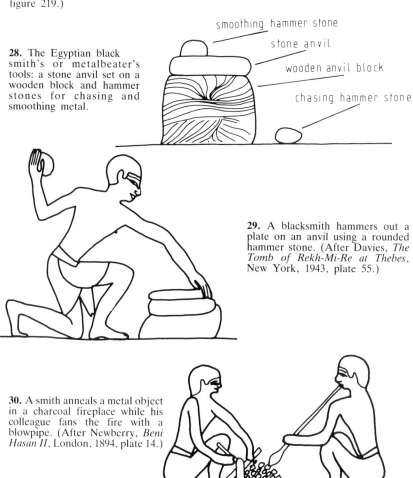

28. The Egyptian black smith's or metalbeater's tools: a stone anvil set on a wooden block and hammer stones for chasing and smoothing metal.

smoothing hammer stone

stone anvil

wooden anvil block

chasing hammer stone

29. A blacksmith hammers out a plate on an anvil using a rounded hammer stone. (After Davies, *The Tomb of Rekh-Mi-Re at Thebes*, New York, 1943, plate 55.)

30. A smith anneals a metal object in a charcoal fireplace while his colleague fans the fire with a blowpipe. (After Newberry, *Beni Hasan II*, London, 1894, plate 14.)

or thick objects had to be annealed, it might be necessary to use the more effective dish bellows for blowing air into the glowing charcoal, as shown on wall paintings in the Eighteenth Dynasty tomb of the Vizier Hepu at Thebes (figure 32).

Gold leaf

The wall painting in the tomb of Rekhmire depicts, beside the brazier, the tools used for the production of gold leaf (figure 31). On a stone block layers of thin gold plates and gold beater's skins are ready for the beating of gold leaf (figure 33). The gold beaters also used hammer stones to beat the foil, which became thinner in the course of the manufacturing process. Silver and electrum also were worked to foil, or the thinnest leaf thickness. Objects of a

31. (Left) A smith works at a brazier to anneal a metal object. (After Davies, *The Tomb of Rekh-Mi-Re at Thebes*, New York, 1943, plate 55.)

32. (Right) A smith anneals a metal object in a fireplace which is fanned by dish bellows. (After Davies, *Scenes from Some Theban Tombs*, Private Tombs at Thebes IV, Oxford, 1963, plate 8.)

less rare material were often gilded or silver-plated. Gold, silver and electrum foils or leaves could be used to cover wooden furniture, statues, coffins and models of daily life manufactured for funerary equipment. Stone vessels, the walls and doors of temples and objects of base metal were covered with precious metal by wrapping the foil round the edge of the object or by inserting the edges of the foil into grooves cut in the surface of the underlying material. In New Kingdom times or even earlier, Egyptian metallurgists mastered advanced techniques of gold refining in order to produce very pure gold, free of impurities, which would be beaten out to the thinnest gold leaf.

The thinner gold leaf could be stuck to surfaces with an adhesive. For the decoration of wooden or stone objects with gold leaf a ground of gypsum plaster or a similar material was often applied first to the material before the gold leaf was stuck to it. It seems probable that metalworkers only produced the gold leaf while the gilding was done by the workers in wood, stone or wax who manufactured the objects to be gilded.

As described in an Egyptian papyrus of the Roman Period, metal-gilders of that time knew the chemical process of fire-gilding with gold amalgam. Gold amalgam was applied to the base-metal object to be gilded. In the course of the fire-gilding process the mercury content of the gold amalgam vaporised and the gold remained on the surface of the metal objects. As mercury fumes are extremely toxic, fire-gilders or those living in the neighbourbood of a gilding workshop were always in danger of mercury poisoning.

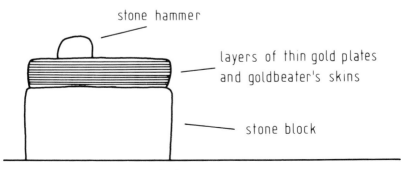

33. Instruments for beating gold leaf.

4
Funerary equipment
and other items

After the plates had been beaten out to workable sheet-metal by the blacksmiths, the whitesmiths (the finishers) received the material for further treatment. Whitesmiths, goldsmiths, silver-smiths and coppersmiths of the temple and palace workshops produced funerary equipment and elaborate objects for daily use. Precious and rare metals such as gold, silver and electrum were needed mainly for the production of vessels and other items intended for use in the royal palace, in temples or as funerary equipment for royal, noble or specially honoured persons. The most common metals or alloys for vessels or other items of daily use were copper, arsenic copper, tin bronze and leaded tin bronze. From Early Dynastic times to the Graeco-Roman Period there was a great demand for bowls, ewers, vases and other kinds of vessels.

The first depiction of the manufacture of a libation vessel appears on a relief in the Fourth Dynasty tomb of the Vizier Nebemakhet, the son of Queen Meresankh III and King Khaefre, at Giza (figure 34). Hand-basins and ewers produced by copper-smiths were very common: nearly every museum with a collection of ancient Egyptian art houses a set of these vessels (figure 35).

Soldering

The spouts of libation vessels or ewers, as well as the specially formed feet, necks and handles of vessels, were made separately and had to be attached to the body of the vessel by riveting, clamping or soldering. Examination of the artefacts shows that Egyptian smiths applied hard soldering with metal alloys, joined above 427 C (800 F). Our present knowledge indicates that the technique of soldering was known in Egypt by the Fourth Dynasty, though Sumerian smiths practised hard soldering much earlier. Thus there is evidence of Sumerian influence on the development of soldering in the Old Kingdom. From the Twelfth Dynasty different mixtures of gold, silver and copper were used to produce solders of different colours and melting points. Natron, a naturally occurring salt, may have been used as flux. Lead-tin solders joined below 427 C (800 F) were known from the Ptolemaic Period. The process of soldering was carried out in

34. (Right) A whitesmith produces a libation vessel from sheet metal. Above the scene a finished vessel is shown. (After Lepsius, *Denkmaeler aus Aegypten und Aethopien III, Abt. II*, Berlin, 1942-5, plate 13.)

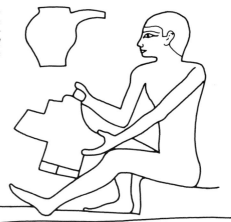

35. (Below) Hand-basin and ewer made of copper, dating from the Old Kingdom. Basin height 12.5 cm (4.9 inches): ewer height 16.8 cm (6.6 inches). (Kestner-Museum, Hanover 1929.618.)

charcoal fireplaces or braziers. The workpieces to be soldered were held together by tongs.

Hammering

Bowls, basins and the bodies of ewers and vases were hammered on special anvils, probably made of wood. On a relief in the Fifth Dynasty tomb of the two overseers of the palace manicurists, Niankhkhnum and Khnumhotep, at Saqqara a metalworker is shown hammering out a sheet of metal to form a hand-basin on a

36. (Left) A whitesmith producing a hand-basin. The hieroglyphic inscription means 'hammering at the bottom'. (After Moussa and Altenmüller, *Das Grab des Nianchchnum and Chnumhotep*, Mainz, 1977, plate 63.)

37. (Right) A smith, using a hammer stone with a flat face, smooths a vessel on a special wooden anvil. (After Davies, *The Tomb of Rekh-Mi-Re at Thebes*, New York, 1943, plate 55.)

wooden anvil consisting of two posts bound together (figure 36). As in the production of plate (chapter 3) the metalworkers used hammer stones with rounded sides for chasing and flat ones for smoothing. In New Kingdom tombs another kind of anvil for vessel production is depicted consisting of a stout pole supported diagonally by a kind of wooden trestle, as shown in the tomb of the Vizier Rekhmire (figure 37).

In the course of chasing, the metal object had to be heated or annealed to improve its ductility. Vessels which were hammered from a single sheet of metal had to be annealed repeatedly. Small flasks hammered from a single sheet of copper or bronze resting in a ring stand (figure 38) were very common from the end of the Middle Kingdom to the Graeco-Roman period. For these objects requiring craftsmanship, the smiths must have used tools much more sophisticated than coarse hammer stones but examples of special metalworker's hammers have not been found or depicted.

Polishing

After the sheet metal had been hammered out and formed into objects these were polished. A wall drawing from the tomb of the Vizier Rekhmire shows a metalworker polishing an offering stand

38. (Left) A small bronze flask and ring stand of the Late Period. Flask height 19.4 cm (7.6 inches). (Kestner-Museum, Hanover 1935.200.743.)

39. (Below) A metalworker polishes an offering stand. (After Davies, *The Tomb of Rekh-Mi-Re at Thebes*, New York, 1943, plate 55.)

(figure 39). On the left behind him are his anvil and finished metal objects, two bowls and a censer with a duck-head handle. Censers were used as part of the ritual during religious ceremonies and cast bronze handles of censers terminating in a falcon head were very common (figure 40). Censers, libation vessels and offering stands of precious metals were made for the offering rituals involved in the worship of the gods; such rituals are shown being performed by the king in the decoration of royal tombs and temples (figure 41). The process of polishing depicted in the tomb of the Vizier Rekhmire is predated by a hieroglyphic inscription on a relief in the causeway leading to the Fifth Dynasty pyramid of King Unas at Saqqara (figure 42).

For polishing, the Egyptian metalworkers used special stones

40. (Above) Cast bronze handle of a censer terminating in a falcon head, Late Period. Length 33.3 cm (13 inches). (Kestner-Museum, Hanover 2557.)

41. (Right) Seti I censing and libating in front of Sokar; relief on a wall of Seti's temple at Abydos. The handle of the censer terminates in a falcon head. (Author's photograph.)

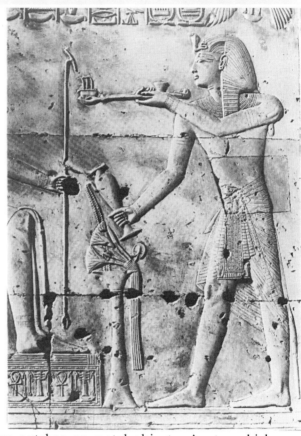

to smooth uneven patches on metal objects. Agate, which was probably used for polishing stones, can be found at several places in Egypt and is still used today for polishing by goldsmiths in Egypt and elsewhere. Metal surfaces may also have been finished using abrasives like emery or sand. The gleaming surfaces on the pieces were obtained by a final burnishing with small balls made

42. Two metalworkers polishing vessels, as written in hieroglyphics above the scene. (After Hassan, 'Excavations at Saqqara 1937-1938', *Annales du service des antiquités de l'Egypte*, 38 (1938), plate 96.)

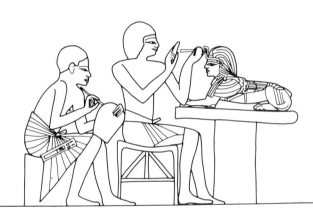

43. A scribe or outline drawer marking a vessel; an engraver is engraving the uraeus of a sphinx. (After Davies, *The Tomb of Two Sculptors at Thebes*, New York, 1925, plate 11.)

44. An engraver is engraving a large metal vase. With his left hand he wields a chisel, with his right hand the engraver's hammer stone. (After Davies, *The Tomb of Rekh-Mi-Re at Thebes*, New York, 1943, plate 55.)

of leather, felt or other textiles.

Engraving

Very precious vessels were often provided with inscriptions or decorations. A scribe or outline drawer sketched the hieroglyphic text or the ornament for the engravers or specially skilled metalworkers. This process is depicted in the Eighteenth Dynasty tomb of the head sculptor of the King, Nebamun, and his fellow sculptor Ipuky at Thebes (figure 43). The engraver worked out the outline drawing using a hammer stone and chisels of different sizes as shown in this tomb or in that of Rekhmire (figure 44). Apart from chasing with hammer and chisels, thus marking without a cutting edge, Egyptian engravers also mastered engraving with gravers, a method of cutting inscriptions or pictures on metal with a chisel-pointed flint tool.

Casting

Other important metallurgical processes included different forms of casting. The first stage was the casting of copper or arsenic copper in simple open moulds: Egyptian founders cut the desired shape in stone or formed it in clay. However, this primitive kind of mould, which was known in Early Dynastic times, was usually utilised only for simple tools or weapons. A much more sophisticated form of casting was developed in the course of the Old Kingdom: the use of two-part moulds. Unlike the primitive open moulds, two-part moulds of clay or stone like steatite or serpentine allowed both faces of the object to be fashioned.

Sumerian founders practised casting a little earlier than their Egyptian counterparts. Open-mould, two-part mould and even lost-wax casting were mastered by Sumerian metalworkers by approximately 3500-3200 BC. Lost-wax casting, often referred to as *cire perdue*, made possible the manufacture of very detailed and complex shapes. In Egypt there is evidence for lost-wax casting in the Old Kingdom and in Middle Kingdom times lost-wax casting was well developed, as is evidenced by items of jewellery, practical objects and statuettes designed for religious purposes (figure 45).

The technique of lost-wax casting required skilled artists, potters and metalworkers. First, an artist, perhaps a sculptor, produced in beeswax a model of the object to be cast. (In early times beeswax was available from wild bees, but by the Old Kingdom apiculture was practised in Egypt.) The beeswax model

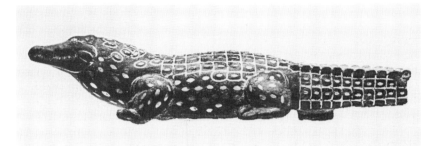

45. The crocodile god Sobek. Manufactured by lost-wax casting using an alloy of copper and lead, the statuette was inlaid with electrum. Length 22.4 cm (8.8 inches). (Staatliche Sammlung Ägyptischer Kunst, Munich ÄS 6080.)

was then coated with clay, probably by a potter. The composite structure was heated in a charcoal fireplace to harden the clay and to melt the wax, so that a clay mould remained retaining every detail of the former wax model. For casting the founder poured the molten metal into the clay mould. After cooling the clay mould was broken and the cast object could be cleaned and polished. For casting jewellery, amulets or other valuable items gold, silver and electrum were used in this way.

The earliest castings were made in copper or arsenic copper alloys, but from the Twelfth Dynasty tin bronze came into increasing use. In New Kingdom times there was an increasing demand for luxury goods, particularly for those associated with personal grooming. Razors, scissors, tweezer-razors, hair-curlers and mirrors were produced in great numbers. The handles of mirrors, in particular, were made by lost-wax casting in the shape of nude young women (figure 46). Both the disc of the mirror and the handle were usually made of bronze. The disc and handle were cast separately and normally riveted together. The disc was polished or plated with a reflecting metal like silver.

From the Late Period to Graeco-Roman times mass-production of figures of deities by lost-wax casting became very common. The small bronze statuettes served as expressions of personal devotion and were often donated to temples as votive offerings (figure 47). The growth of temples led to mass-production in temple workshops where vessels, offering stands and other items for ritual use were produced (figure 48).

To cast larger objects by the lost-wax method using a beeswax model meant the waste of a large amount of useful wax. (Wax was a remedy in ancient Egyptian medicine for internal use, for dressing wounds and for other special purposes.) To fill the large mould completely with bronze also meant a waste of this expensive material. Therefore, the founders started to practise the metallurgical innovation of core casting, which might also have been introduced to Egyptian metalworkers by contacts with Sumerian smiths. Considerably less wax and metal were needed for core casting. A core of clay or sand was covered by a layer of malleable wax shaped to form the mould of the object to be cast. The model, consisting of the core and the formed wax layer, was coated with clay. In order to secure it in position throughout the later casting process, the core had to be stabilised by pins or wire fixed to the outer cover of clay. The wax was melted away leaving in the kiln the hardened clay mould with the fixed core. For casting the piece only the gap between the outer clay mould and the inner core had to be filled with bronze or other molten metal.

46. Bronze mirror with handle in the shape of a nude woman. The handle was produced by lost-wax casting. (Ägyptisches Museum, Berlin SMPK 13187.)

47. (Left) Isis with Horus on her lap. Made of bronze by lost-wax casting, probably Late Period. Height 15.6 cm (6.1 inches). (Kestner-Museum, Hanover 2502.)

48. (Right) Bronze ram's head finial, probably to be attached to a staff or piece of temple furniture. Made by lost-wax casting and engraved. Height 10 cm (3.9 inches). (Kestner-Museum, Hanover 1935.200.579.)

After cooling the mould was broken and as far as possible the core was removed from the cast object. Core casting was very common in the manufacture of larger objects during the New Kingdom and reached its peak in the Late Period.

Wirework and jewellery

The metalworkers produced wires of gold, silver or bronze for particular purposes. Plain wire appeared in the First Dynasty and was used for the construction and repair of furniture or for fastening building ornaments like wall tiles of blue or green faience in temples or palaces. The most famous are the riveted tile walls inside the underground rooms of the Third Dynasty step pyramid complex of King Djoser at Saqqara.

Hand-made wire could be produced by different methods. The simplest, most common and probably the oldest method was by hammering. An ingot was hammered out to sheet metal, which was cut into thin strips. These strips were hammered out and cut again. Hammered wires show variations in diameter along the length, a faceted surface and a solid but non-circular cross-section. The faceted surface could be eliminated by rolling the wire between two flat pieces of hard wood. This process of hammering could be used only for the manufacture of relatively thick wires.

Another technique of wire production which is attested to by New Kingdom artefacts is the block-twisting method. An ingot was hammered out to produce a rod of the required thickness for the wire. The rod, which had a square section, was twisted about its major axis to form a solid wire with a screw thread of variable pitch. In the course of this twisting process the wire had to be annealed repeatedly to preserve its ductility. The spiralling could be eliminated by rolling the wire between two flat pieces of hard wood, as mentioned above, for the final stage of the hammering process. The wire could be made thinner by further twisting, stretching and rolling.

In addition to hammering and block-twisting, strip-drawing and strip-twisting were probably mastered by Egyptian wire-makers. For the manufacture of wire by strip-drawing, a strip of metal foil was drawn through a number of holes of different diameters so that the strip curled in upon itself, forming a hollow tube. The strip could have been drawn through holes drilled through precious stones. Egyptian craftsmen had mastered the drilling of stones in Predynastic times and the first depictions of the drilling of precious stones date from the Old Kingdom (figure 49).

For strip-twisting the wire-maker had to cut a strip of metal foil and wrap it around an existing wire (which was removed after this process). The helix was then tightened and stretched out by hand. In the final stage of wire production by this method, the wire could be drawn through holes of different diameters.

Another method of making wires is known from the Nineteenth Dynasty. Granules of metal were soldered together to form a beaded wire which was straightened by rolling it between two flat pieces of wood.

Wires were produced by goldsmiths and silversmiths, by spec-ialised metalworkers or by jewellers. Goldsmiths, silversmiths

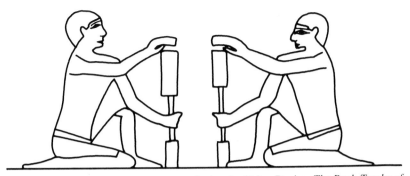

49. Jewellers drilling precious stones to make beads. (After Davies, *The Rock Tombs of Deir el Gebrâwi I*, London, 1902, plate 14.)

and jewellers used wires of precious metal for the decoration of valuable objects or for the manufacture of pieces of jewellery, such as anklets, aprons, armlets, belts, collars, chains, necklaces and pectorals (figure 50). Although the much more specialised skills of the goldsmiths, silversmiths and jewellers will not be discussed in depth here, some of their techniques need to be mentioned because metalworkers producing ordinary vessels and

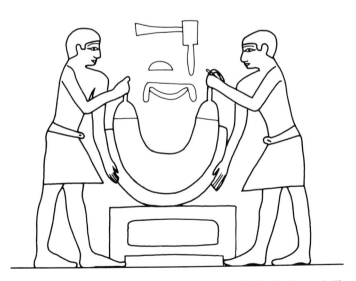

50. Two jewellers looking at a finished collar. The hieroglyphic inscription reads 'Knotting of the collar'. (After Moussa and Altenmüller, *Das Grab des Nianchchnum und Chnumhotep*, Mainz, 1977, plate 64.)

other items also made use of these techniques occasionally.

Filigree was delicate ornamental wirework in which ornaments were formed by bending all kinds of wire to form a delicate tracery. The shaped pieces of wire were soldered together. Filigree was used for jewellery or could be fixed by soldering to other decorative items.

Cloisonné was another ornamental process, in which sections were formed by bending round thin strips of metal. Placed on edge and soldered to base plates, they formed cells or *cloisons* which were filled with coloured inlays.

Repoussé work facilitated the manufacture of raised reliefs. *Repoussé* may be regarded as the complementary process to chasing, taking place on the back of the metal sheet instead of its face. The sheet was fastened to a soft base so that the back of the metal object could be worked with suitable tools made of bone, hardwood, stone or metal.

Egyptian jewellers were skilled in many other decorative and ornamental techniques. Their colleagues, the metalworkers and smiths, restricted themselves to the skills described above: forms of gilding, silver-plating and alloying of precious metals.

5
Tools and their uses

Apart from the manufacture of temple, palace and funerary equipment, the skills of Egyptian metalworkers were also very important in other fields of activity. Craftsmen like joiners, carpenters, shipwrights, wood sculptors or carvers, stonemasons, quarry workers, stone sculptors, leather-workers and textile workers needed the tools produced by metalworkers. Not only craftsmen were dependent on metal tools — barbers, manicurists, doctors, agricultural workers, butchers and many others used metal tools and other items designed for particular purposes.

Axes, adzes and saws
The axe was one of the most important tools for Egyptian craftsmen engaged in woodworking. From the late Predynastic Period to Graeco-Roman times different types of blade were fitted to the Egyptian axe (figure 51). The first flat blades were made of native copper or copper with a natural content of arsenic. The equal-faced blades were shaped and hardened by hammering, especially at the edges. At the beginning of the Dynastic Period, or even earlier, copper blades were produced by open-mould casting. The edges of the relatively thick and heavy blades then produced also had to be shaped and hardened by hammering. From the Twelfth Dynasty, imports of tin bronze led to the casting of bronze blades. From the Late Period, or occasionally earlier, iron blades were used. The earliest forms of metal blades were very similar to stone axes. Metal axes from the beginning of the Dynastic Period do not have any special attachments for handles and their cutting edge has a semicircular outline. Another type of blade without attachments from the early Dynastic Period is a tapered form resembling a trapezium.
  In the Sixth Dynasty axe blades were produced with lugs at their sides, which enabled the axe to be more firmly and easily fastened to the handle. The laterally projecting lugs were fitted into a grooved wooden handle. To fasten the blade parallel to the handle, a wet leather lashing was wound and woven around the handle lugs. When it dried, the leather lashing tightened by shrinking. Semicircular axes with lugs lasted into the Eighteenth Dynasty, if only for ceremonial purposes. From New Kingdom times axes with trapeziform blades and strongly marked side attachments became common.

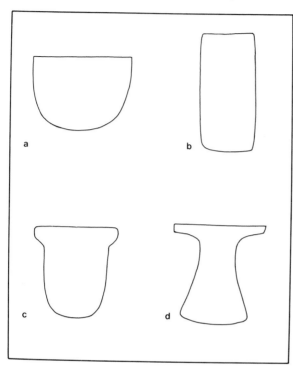

51. Different types of blade in Egyptian axes: a. Old Kingdom axe-blade with semicircular shape, length 9.6 cm; b. Old Kingdom axe-blade resembling a trapezium, length 12.0 cm; c. Sixth Dynasty axe-blade with lugs, length 4.8 cm; d. New Kingdom trapeziform axe-blade, length 10.4 cm. (After Petrie, *Tools and Weapons*, London, 1917, plates 2, 3, 4.)

Several other blade forms are known from Egypt but those mentioned above are the most important. To cut down trees the woodcutter's axe had a long handle and was wielded with both hands (figure 52). Carpenters and shipwrights needed axes for rough work such as the splitting of logs. There is no evidence that

52. Woodcutter at work. The blade of his axe is semicircular. (After Moussa and Altenmüller, *The Tomb of Nefer and Kahay*, Mainz 1971, plate 22b.)

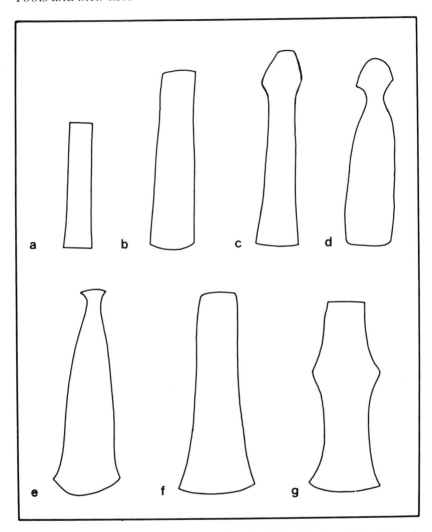

53. Different types of adze-blade: a. Narrow thin adze-blade of Predynastic Egypt, length 8.0 cm; b. Early Dynastic adze-blade, length 17.4 cm; c. Third Dynasty adze-blade with a marked notch in the upper end, length 21.0 cm; d. Fourth or Fifth Dynasty adze-blade with a clearly formed head, length 19.0 cm; e. Twelfth Dynasty adze-blade showing a degradation in the head, length 18.4 cm; f. Eighteenth Dynasty adze-blade without head, length 18.2 cm; g. Adze-blade of the Third Intermediate Period with side protrusions, length 16.0 cm. (After Petrie, *Tools and Weapons*, London, 1917, plates 16, 17.)

Egyptian joiners, carpenters or shipwrights ever used hatchets
with blades fastened parallel to the handles. Instead, they worked
with a similar tool, the adze. The adze blade was fastened across
the top of a short wooden handle with leather thongs. From
Predynastic times to the Graeco-Roman Period several forms of
adze-blade with parallel sides are known. Long, narrow copper
blades with parallel sides have been found from Predynastic
Egypt. Early Dynastic blades became broader at the lower end
and slightly concave at the sides. From the Second Dynasty a type
of blade with a rounded upper end developed. From the Third
Dynasty blades with a marked notch in the upper end were used.
This type developed much further in the Fourth and Fifth
Dynasties to a clearly formed head. In the Twelfth Dynasty
bronze blades were used as well as copper ones and in the
Eighteenth Dynasty blades without a head became common. In
the Third Intermediate Period a new type was introduced which
had side protrusions, or lugs, for the leather lashing. The adze
was needed for many kinds of woodworking, such as planing,
shown in a wall painting from the tomb of Nebamun and Ipuky
(figure 54).

The metal saw was already known at the beginning of the First
Dynasty. Saws of different types and sizes, with or without
wooden handles, were used throughout Egyptian history for the
production of boards, planks and veneers. The saw blades were
made of copper or sometimes, from the Twelfth Dynasty, of
bronze. Saw blades were hammered out by metalworkers. The

54. A carpenter working with an adze. (After
Davies, *The Tomb of Two Sculptors at Thebes*,
New York, 1925, plate 11.)

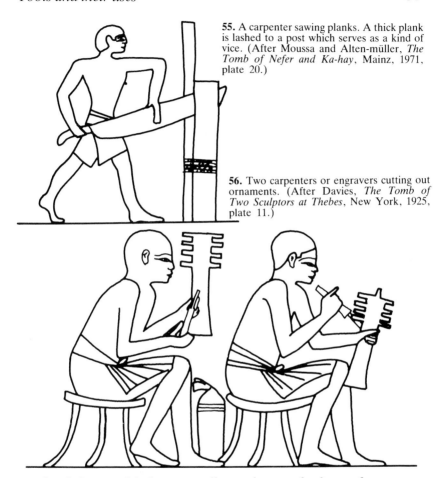

55. A carpenter sawing planks. A thick plank is lashed to a post which serves as a kind of vice. (After Moussa and Alten-müller, *The Tomb of Nefer and Ka-hay*, Mainz, 1971, plate 20.)

56. Two carpenters or engravers cutting out ornaments. (After Davies, *The Tomb of Two Sculptors at Thebes*, New York, 1925, plate 11.)

teeth of the saw blades were directed towards the craftsman, so that Egyptian saws had to be drawn backwards. Logs or thick planks were often lashed to a post struck into the ground, which served as a kind of vice (figure 55). Large saws for board or veneer production were worked with both hands, while smaller saws for precision work were wielded with one hand.

Other important tools for woodworking were chisels and engravers, produced by open-mould or two-part mould casting in the metal workshops. Chisels and engravers of several sizes and kinds were needed by woodworkers to carve decoration and for other special purposes (figure 56).

The blades of all these tools were formed by hammering and in

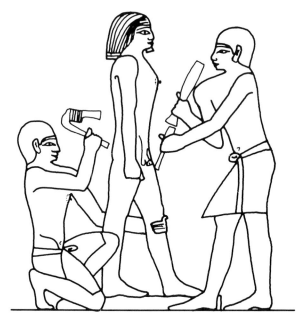

57. Two wood sculptors working at a statue. Their tools are an adze, a chisel and a mallet. (After Wild, *Le Tombeau de Ti*, Cairo, 1939, plate 173.)

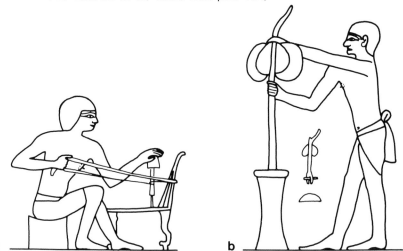

a   b

58. Drilling of wood and stone. a. A carpenter using a bow-drill; b. A stoneworker using a drill with a special crank to hollow out a stone vessel. (After Davies, *The Tomb of Rekh-Mi-Re at Thebes*, New York, 1942, plate 52, and Wild, *Le Tombeau de Ti*, Cairo, 1939, plate 173.)

the course of manufacturing they all had to be annealed. The cutting edges were sharpened using a kind of whetstone.

Egyptian wood sculptors used nearly the same tools as their colleagues the carpenters, joiners and shipwrights (figure 57): the adze, the chisel with a sharp cutting edge and the mallet were their specific tools.

Stoneworkers' tools

Egyptian quarrymen, stone cutters, stonemasons and stone sculptors were using large copper saws for stonecutting by Old Kingdom times. Metal wedges were used for splitting blocks of stone. Bronze wedges dating to the Saite Period (Twenty-sixth Dynasty) and others made of iron dating from the Late Period are known from the sites of Tell Defenna and Naucratis in the Delta and from the mortuary temple of the Pharaoh Ramesses II in Thebes. While woodworkers used sharpened chisels fixed to a wooden handle, stoneworkers usually used relatively blunt chisels without special handles to carve all kinds of stone.

Drills

For the drilling of holes or hollows stoneworkers and wood-workers used special drills. Metal drills were in use by Old Kingdom times. The so-called bow-drill, used in woodworking, was constructed using a wooden shaft, the drill stock, with a stone or, more effectively, a metal bit, at the lower shaft end. The upper end of the shaft was covered with a rounded drill-cap (figure 58). With his left hand on the drill-cap the craftsman held the drill stock in position and applied the necessary pressure to the shaft. With his right hand the worker wielded the bow, the string of which caused the drill stock to rotate. The metal bits were produced by hammering or casting small quantities of copper, bronze or even iron.

Stoneworkers used another kind of drill with a crank upon the drill-cap. Instead of the drill-cap, heavy stones could be used to apply the required pressure to the wooden shaft. Stone vessels were hollowed out by using drills fitted with stone and metal bits or with special tubular bits made of copper (figure 58). After drilling with the tubular copper bits cylindrical stone cores remained inside the vessels, which could then easily be chiselled out. The use of these metal bits saved a great deal of time and energy.

With these metal tools stone and wood sculptors made statues and statuettes of deities for ritual use in temples and produced statues of tomb owners and their families for the later cult of the dead. Carpenters used metal tools for the production of furniture, everyday objects and funerary equipment. Chairs, stools, tables, headrests, scales, sticks, combs, hairpins, boxes, spoons, dishes, coffins and shrines were made of wood.

Leather-working tools

Another group of craftsmen who needed metal tools were leather-workers. Tanners and saddlers worked with metal hide-scrapers, leather-cutting knives, awls and needles. As these activities are depicted in the wall paintings and reliefs of private tombs from the Old Kingdom to the Late Period, the manufacture of sandals and leather straps would seem to have been very important to the tomb owners (figure 59).

The leather-cutting knife consisted of a blade and a wooden handle. The copper or bronze blade usually had a wide, splayed convex edge and was inserted into a rounded handle. From the New Kingdom knives with a T-shaped and broader blade are also known.

Saddlers cut out straps of different lengths, which were used to cover wooden stools, for the lashings of tools like axes and adzes and for chariot equipment, including harnesses and whips. For sandal-making square pieces of leather were formed into soles by means of the leather-cutting knife. The soles were pierced by awls so that the thongs could pass through. The leather-worker's metal tools were also used to produce leather ropes, writing materials, quivers, kilts, tents and many other useful items.

59. Leather-workers: (a) making sandals, and (b) making leather straps. (After Davies, *The Tomb of Rekh-Mi-Re* at Thebes, New York, 1943, plate 53.)

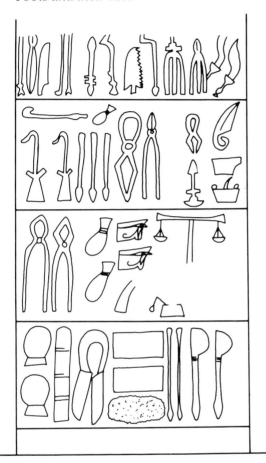

60. A box with medical instruments, of the Roman Period, as depicted on a wall of the Graeco-Roman temple of Kom Ombo.

Dressmaking tools

Egyptian dressmakers and textile workers possessed only a few metal tools. Needles, pins and cutting-out tools for linen were known. Cutting-out knives are often found in the burials of women; the earliest examples can be dated to the First Dynasty. Needles and pins made of copper have been found from Predynastic times. Textile workers' bronze tools are known from the Middle Kingdom and later. Scissors worked by separate fingers were not used before the first century AD but shears, which are similar tools, were known a little earlier, probably in Ptolemaic times.

Agricultural tools

Egyptian agricultural workers used only a limited range of metal tools. Cast bronze hoes were used from the New Kingdom and sickles with edges made of steel are known from Roman Egypt. For a long time, however, agricultural workers used their traditional wood tools: up to New Kingdom times and even later wooden sickles were still equipped with serrated flint blades. In Graeco-Roman Egypt metal implements became much more common. New metal tools were imported from Greece and the Roman Empire and Egyptian metalworkers also copied them.

Medical instruments

As part of a wall decoration in the Graeco-Roman temple of Kom Ombo there is a unique picture of a tall box placed on a stand. Inside the box, a doctor's instruments of the Roman Period are depicted and include metal instruments for surgery, dentistry, gynaecology and general medicine (figure 60): as well as shears, surgical knives and saws, different kinds of probes and spatulas, small hooks and forceps.

Other metal implements

Simple implements such as the blades of knives could have been produced by hammering out a suitable metal plate. More complicated objects such as specially formed spatulas would have had to be cast with a two-part mould or even by the lost-wax method.

A large variety of metal knives was used throughout the history of ancient Egypt from Early Dynastic to Graeco-Roman times. The blades were hammered out from copper plates or made of bronze. Knives were used as weapons and as tools, especially by butchers.

The earliest evidence for the use of tongs appears in metalworking scenes in the New Kingdom tomb of the Vizier Rekhmire (figure 31), or possibly earlier in the Middle Kingdom tomb of the nomarch Khety of the Twelfth Dynasty (figure 30). These lifting tongs were used to hold metal objects in position for annealing in a fireplace. Tongs with special forms of jaw to hold objects or well developed surgical forceps like those depicted in Kom Ombo were not known before the Roman Period.

For personal hygiene or beauty treatment metalworkers manufactured remarkable implements in copper or bronze. Razors, tweezers and special toilet implements, such as tweezer-razors or hair-curlers, were in great demand. Shaggy beards and overall

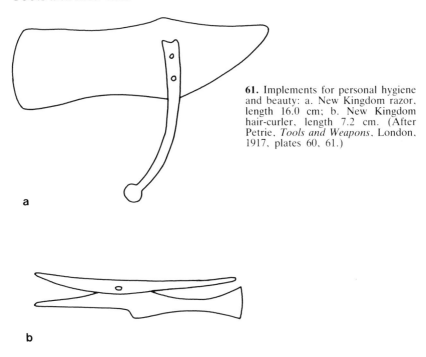

61. Implements for personal hygiene and beauty: a. New Kingdom razor, length 16.0 cm; b. New Kingdom hair-curler, length 7.2 cm. (After Petrie, *Tools and Weapons*, London, 1917, plates 60, 61.)

a

b

hairiness were a sign of slovenliness for the ancient Egyptians, so people who attached importance to personal hygiene shaved their faces, necks, armpits, limbs, chest and pubic regions. Metal razors are known from the late Predynastic Period. Several types were in use from the earliest times to the Graeco-Roman Period. The well developed razors of the New Kingdom consisted of two parts (figure 61): a large thin blade with a convex cutting edge, to which was fixed a handle at right angles from the point formed by the tapered sides of the blade. Handles of wood, metal or other suitable materials were used. Razors produced for royal use or as burial objects were made of gold.

There were many varieties of hair-curlers or tweezer-razors. In general they consisted of two parts: a small knife and a specially formed handle. Both parts were held together by a central pin and could be opened like scissors and clamped together as a hair-curler. The earliest examples of these toilet implements date from the end of the Old Kingdom, but the most beautiful and most versatile ones are from the New Kingdom (figure 61). Tweezers were made with both blunt and sharp ends for different functions. Tweezers with blunt ends could have been used for pulling out hairs while the second type were suitable for extracting thorns from the flesh. The first examples of copper tweezers date from the mid First Dynasty. Bronze tweezers appeared at the beginning of the Middle Kingdom.

There were many other types of metal tools and only the most important have been mentioned here. Weapons and their use in warfare have not been discussed because the production of weapons was not carried out by metalworkers but by specially trained armourers.

6
The social status and organisation of metalworkers

With priests, officials or civil servants, agricultural workers and soldiers, craftsmen formed one of the major occupational groups in ancient Egypt.

The single trades, such as the leather-workers, woodworkers, stoneworkers, potters or metalworkers, were strictly organised. 'Inspectors' supervised the work of a small group of craftsmen belonging to a special trade and the inspectors received their instructions from an overseer. The overseers of the different trades belonging to a large workshop were directed by an 'overseer of the workshop'. Overseers or other persons of high rank are depicted on wall paintings or reliefs in private tombs wearing a long tunic with an underskirt (figure 12). Overseers shown at work are usually distinguished from other craftsmen by the overseer's mace in their hands (figure 11).

A workshop could be attached to a temple, to a royal palace, to the private household of a king's son or to the household of a high official or a nomarch. There were also royal craftsmen who did not belong to the state-owned palace workshop but were part of the private household of the king. As a special honour the king could delegate his own or the palace craftsmen to work for private individuals for a specified time. The craftsmen of palace and temple workshops could also be released for labour in private households.

There were no independent craftsmen with their own workshops and raw materials in ancient Egypt: craftsmen were all dependent on their employers, who kept and allocated the raw materials. Egyptian officials and civil servants were set in authority over the craftsmen. For this reason the officials, and especially the well educated Egyptian scribes, displayed a self-confident status consciousness, as is illustrated by the instructions of a father named Khety to his son Pepi, dating from the early Twelfth Dynasty. Khety wants his son to become an official; he tells him to work hard at school, otherwise he will not be able to become an official and will have to work hard as a craftsman all his life. Khety tries to convince Pepi that a craftsman's trade has enormous disadvantages compared to the pleasant occupation of an official. He tells his son about the different trades and says of metalworkers that he never saw a goldsmith on important business. In contrast, the metalworker was seen at the smelting furnace and because of his work his hands were wrinkled like crocodile skin and he stank worse than scraps of fish. Although Khety's opinion is probably an exaggeration, it does indicate the hard conditions endured by ancient Egyptian metalworkers.

As metalworking was mainly heavy labour, only men practised the trade. They worked collectively in a team of skilled and unskilled workers. In the workshops unskilled workers were employed for work not requiring a specialised knowledge of metallurgy: fanning fires by means of blowpipes or bellows, pouring out the molten metal into open moulds for cooling, or cleaning and polishing vessels.

The skilled workers included blacksmiths, whitesmiths, goldsmiths, silversmiths, engravers and gilders. In contrast with the unskilled workers, who mainly had to show stamina and physical strength, the skilled metalworkers were knowledgeable about metallurgical processes such as chasing, annealing or casting metal. Amongst the skilled metalworkers, the inspectors and overseers had a higher social status than their colleagues without any titles.

The ancient Egyptians also made a distinction between metalworkers who were attached to the royal palace or to a temple workshop and those who worked in the private household of a high official or a nomarch. Naturally, the king or the palace administration had the right (and the resources) to choose the best craftsmen in the country, so metalworkers of the palace workshop enjoyed a higher rank than their colleagues attached to a temple or official's workshop. Royal or palace craftsmen received better wages than those in private households.

Egyptian metalworkers had a special relationship with the Memphite god Sokar, while, as their creator, Ptah of Memphis was responsible for all craftsmen and was worshipped as their patron deity. It was believed that Sokar helped and protected metalworkers in carrying out their profession. Sometimes Sokar was asked for beer by the melters who had to work at the oppressively hot fire. Beer was important in ancient Egypt and was used as payment for workers and labourers. Depending on their rank and social status Egyptian metalworkers were provided with all the goods necessary to sustain life. As well as beer they received grain, bread, cakes, meat, salt, vegetables, dates, sandals and clothing.

7
Glossary

Amalgam: an alloy containing mercury.

Azurite: copper ore, a basic copper carbonate. Its vivid blue colour contrasts strikingly with the emerald-green malachite it usually accompanies. The formula is $2Cu\,CO_3.\,Cu(OH)_2$.

Cassiterite: a mineral from which most of the world's tin is obtained, also known as tinstone. It is usually brown or black, occasionally yellow or white. The streak is white. Composed of tin dioxide, formula SnO_2.

Cementation: metallurgical process for obtaining a metal from solution through displacement by a more active metal.

Charge: the mixture of charcoal and ore loaded into a smelting furnace.

Chrysocolla: copper ore, a green or blue-green copper silicate. The formula is $Cu\,SiO_3$ + aq.

Cupellation: metallurgical process for separating precious metals from base metals.

Galena: a major lead ore; a lead sulphide. The mineral and its streak are lead-grey. The formula is PbS.

Gangue: associated minerals of an ore, non-metalliferous or non-valuable metalliferous.

Haematite: most important iron ore, consisting of ferric oxide with steel-grey crystals and a red-brown streak. The formula is F_2O_3.

Limonite: a natural hydrated ferric oxide found mainly as earthy or porous masses, brown to yellow in colour (yellow ochre). The streak is yellow-brown. The formula is $Fe_2\,O_3.\,H_2O$.

Magnetite: important iron ore, a black opaque mineral with metallic lustre. The streak is black. The formula is Fe_3O_4 or $FeFe_2O_4$.

Malachite: bright green copper ore; a basic copper carbonate. The formula is $CuCO_3Cu(OH)_2$.

Pyrites: also known as fool's gold: a naturally occurring iron disulphide. The formula is FeS_2.

8
Museums

Nearly every museum with an Egyptology collection exhibits metal objects or tools. Only the most important museums are therefore named below. Intending visitors are advised to ascertain the opening times before making a special journey.

United Kingdom

Ashmolean Museum of Art and Archaeology, Beaumont Street, Oxford OX1 2PH. Telephone: 0865 278000.

Bolton Museum and Art Gallery, Le Mans Crescent, Bolton, Lancashire BL1 1SE. Telephone: 0204 22311, extension 2191.

British Museum, Great Russell Street, London WC1B 3DG. Telephone: 01-636 1555 or 1558.

Fitzwilliam Museum, Trumpington Street, Cambridge CB2 1RB. Telephone: 0223 332900.

Manchester Museum, The University of Manchester, Oxford Road, Manchester M13 9PL. Telephone: 061-275 2634.

Petrie Museum of Egyptian Archaeology, University College London, Gower Street, London WC1E 6BT. Telephone: 01-387 7050, extension 2884.

Royal Museum of Scotland, Chambers Street, Edinburgh EH1 1JF. Telephone: 031-225 7534.

Austria

Kunsthistorisches Museum, Ägyptisch-Orientalische Sammlung, Burgring 5, 1010 Vienna.

Belgium

Musées Royaux d'Art et d'Histoire, Avenue J. F. Kennedy, 1040 Brussels.

Canada

Royal Ontario Museum, 100 Queen's Park, Toronto, Ontario M5C 2C6.

Denmark

Ny Carlsberg Glyptotek, Dantes Plads, 1550 Copenhagen V.

Egypt

Egyptian Antiquities Museum, Tahrir Square, Cairo.

France
Musée du Louvre, Palais du Louvre, 75003 Paris.

Germany, East
Ägyptisches Museum and Papyrus-sammlung, Staatliche Museen zu Berlin, Bodestrasse 1-3, 102 Berlin.
Karl-Marx-Universität, Sektion Afrika- und Nahost-wissenschaften, Bereich, Ägyptologie und Ägyptisches Museum, Schillerstrasse 6, 701 Leipzig.

Germany, West
Ägyptisches Museum, Staatliche Museen Preussischer Kulturbesitz, Schlossstrasse 70, 1000 Berlin 19.
Kestner-Museum, Trammplatz 3, 3000 Hanover 1.
Roemer-Pelizaeus-Museum, Am Steine 1-2, 3200 Hildesheim, Niedersachsen.
Staatliche Sammlung Ägyptischer Kunst, Meiserstrasse 10, 8000 Munich 2.

Italy
Museo Archeologico, Via Colonna 96, Florence.
Museo Egizio, Palazzo dell'Accademia delle Scienze, Via Accademia delle Scienze 6, Turin.

Netherlands
Rijiksmuseum van Oudheden, Rapenburg 28, 2311 EW, Leiden.

United States of America
Brooklyn Museum, 188 Eastern Parkway, Brooklyn, New York, NY 11238.
Metropolitan Museum of Art, 5th Avenue at 82nd Street, New York, NY 10028.
Museum of Fine Arts, Huntington Avenue, Boston, Massachusetts 02115.
University of Chicago Oriental Institute Museum, 1155 East 58th Street, Chicago, Illinois 60637.
Yale University Art Gallery, 1111 Chapel Street, New Haven, Connecticut 06520.

9
Further reading

Aldred, C. *Jewels of the Pharaohs. Egyptian Jewellery of the Dynastic Period.* Thames and Hudson, London, 1971.

Baines, J., and Málek, J. *Atlas of Ancient Egypt.* Phaidon, Oxford, 1980.

Chappaz, J.-L. 'La Purification de l'Or', *Bulletin de la Société d'Égyptologie de Genève,* 4 (1980), 19-24.

Cowell, M. 'The Composition of Egyptian Copper-based Metalwork' in R. A. David (editor), *Science in Egyptology,* Manchester University Press, Manchester, 1986.

Davey, C. J. 'Crucibles in the Petrie Collection and Hieroglyphic Ideograms for Metal', *Journal of Egyptian Archaeology,* 71 (1985), 142-8.

Dayton, J. *Minerals, Metals, Glazing and Man or Who was Sesostris I?* Harrap, London, 1978.

Drenkhahn, R. *Die Handwerker und ihre Tätigkeiten im Alten Ägypten.* Ägyptologische Abhandlungen 31, Harrassowitz, Wiesbaden, 1976.

Forbes, R. J. *Metallurgy in Antiquity. A Notebook for Archaeologists and Technologists.* Brill, Leiden, 1950.

Forbes, R. J. *Studies in Ancient Technology,* volumes VI-IX. Brill, Leiden, 1966, 1971 and 1972.

Harris, J. R. *Lexicographical Studies in Ancient Egyptian Minerals.* Veröffentlichung 54, Deutsche Akademie der Wissenschaften zu Berlin, Institut für Orientforschung, Berlin, 1961.

Helck, W. *Die Beziehungen Ägyptens zu Vorderasien im 3. u. 2. Jahrtausend v. Chr.* Ägyptologische Abhandlungen 5, Harrassowitz, Wiesbaden, 1962.

Hunt, L. B. 'The Long History of Lost Wax Casting. Over Five Thousand Years of Art and Craftsmanship', *Gold Bulletin,* 13, 2 (1980), 63-79.

James, T. G. H. 'Gold Technology in Ancient Egypt. Mastery of Metal Working Methods', *Gold Bulletin,* 5, 2 (1972), 38-42.

Kense, F. J. *Traditional African Iron Working.* African Occasional Papers, University of Calgary Press, Calgary, 1983.

Leclant, J. 'Le Fer dans l'Egypte ancienne, le Soudan et l'Afrique', *Annales de l'Est, publiées par la faculté des lettres de l'Université de Nancy,* Mémoire 16 (1956), 83-91.

Lucas, A. *Ancient Egyptian Materials and Industries.* J. R. Harris (editor). Arnold, London, fourth edition, 1962.

Maddin, R. 'Early Iron Metallurgy in the Near East', *Transactions of the Iron and Steel Institute of Japan*, 15, 2 (1975), 59-68.

Moesta, H. *Erze und Metalle ihre Kulturgeschichte im Experiment.* Springer-Verlag, Berlin, Heidelberg, New York, 1983.

Muhly, J. D. 'Timna and King Solomon', *Bibliotheca Orientalis*, 41, 3 and 4 (1984), 275-92.

Nibbi, A. *Ancient Egyptian Pot Bellows and the Oxhide Ingot Shape.* Discussion in Egyptology Publications, Oxford, 1987.

Notton, J. H. F. 'Ancient Egyptian Gold Refining. A Reproduction of Early Techniques', *Gold Bulletin*, 7, 2 (1974), 50-6.

Petrie, W. M. Flinders. *Tools and Weapons.* British School of Archaeology in Egypt, University College, London, 1917.

Petruso, K. M. 'Early Weights and Weighing in Egypt and the Indus Valley', *Bulletin of the Museum of Fine Arts*, 79 (1981), 44-51.

Scheel, B. 'Studien zum Metallhandwerk im Alten Ägypten I. Handlungen und Beischriften in den Bildprogrammen der Gräber des Alten Reiches', *Studien zur Altägyptischen Kultur*, 12 (1985), 117-77.

Scheel, B. 'Studien zum Metallhandwerk im Alten Ägypten II. Handlungen und Beischriften in den Bildprogrammen der Gräber des Mittleren Reiches', *Studien zur Altägyptischen Kultur*, 13 (1986), 181-205.

Scheel, B. 'Studien zum Metallhandwerk im Alten Ägypten III. Handlungen und Beischriften in den Bildprogrammen der Gräber des Neuen Reiches und der Spätzeit', *Studien zur Altägyptischen Kultur*, 14 (1987), 247-64.

Tylecote, R. F. 'The Origin of Iron Smelting in Africa', *West African Journal of Archaeology*, 5 (1975), 1-9.

Vercoutter, J. 'The Gold of Kush. Two Gold-washing Stations at Faras East', *Kush. Journal of the Sudan Antiquities Service*, 7 (1959), 120-53.

Weinstein, J. 'A Fifth Dynasty Reference to Annealing', *Journal of the American Research Center in Egypt*, 11 (1974), 23-5.

Whitehouse, D. and R. *Archaeological Atlas of the World.* Thames and Hudson, London, 1975.

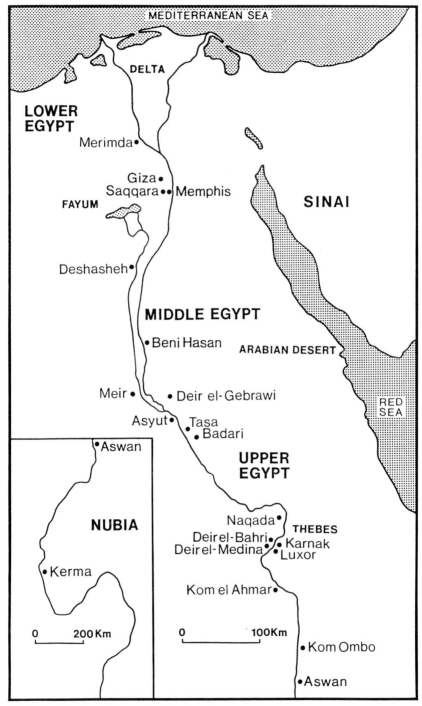

62. Map of ancient Egypt, showing the sites mentioned in the text.

Index

Page numbers in italic refer to illustrations.

Abu Hamed *10*, 11
Administration 9, 14, 21, 60
Adze 18, 47, 50, *50*, 52-4
Agate 38
Agatharchides of Cnidus 11-12, 14, 17
Alalakh 19
Aleppo 19
Alloy 15, 20, 34, 41, *41*
Alloying 19-21, 46
Amenophis II *15*
Amun 24-5
Anatolia 6-8, 17, 19
Annealing 8, 30-1, 36, 44, 53, 56, 60
Antimony 11
Anvil 28, 31, 35, *36*, 36-7
Arsenic 11, 14, 20, 34, 40-1, 47
Aswan 17
Asyut 8
Awl 54
Axe 47, 48, *48*, 54
Badari *6*, 8
Bellows 15-16, 23-5, 27, 32, 60
Bending 8, 46
Beni Suef 14
Berenike 14
Blacksmith 28, 30-1, 34, 60
Blowpipe *9*, 22-4, *24*, 30-1, 60
Bowl furnace 15, *16*
Brazier 30, 32, 35
Bronze *see* Tin bronze
Buhen *10*, 11
Byblos 19
Casting 8-9, 19-21, 24, 25, *25*, 27, 29, 40-3, 47, 51, 53, 56, 60
Çatal Hüyük *6*, 7
Çaucasus 19
Çayönü Tepesi *6*, 7
Charcoal 9, *9*, 15, 23-5, 27, 30-2, 35, 41
Chasing 28, 30-1, 36, 40, 46, 60
Chisels *39*, 40, 51, *52*, 53
Cire perdue 40
Clamping 34, 57
Cloisonné work 46
Cobalt 11
Copper 7-9, 11, 14, 19-21, 34-5, 40, 41, *41*, 47, 50, 53-6, 58
Crete 17-18
Crucible *9*, 22, *22*, 23, *23*, 24, 25, 27-8, 30
Curlers 41, 56, 57, *57*
Cutting 8, 40, 44, *51*, 54
Cyprus 14, 17-18, 20
Defennah 17, 53
Djoser 44
Drills *45*, *52*, 53
Eilat 14

Electrum 11, 15-16, 32, 34, 41, *41*
Engraver *39*, 40, 51, 60
Engraving *39*, 40, *43*
Euphrates *6*, 8
Fans *22*, 23
Fayum 8
Filigree 46
Fireplace *9*, *22-3*, 23-4, 30-1, 35, 41, 56
Forceps 56
Foundry 24-5, *26*
Funerary equipment *13*, 14, 16, 21, 32, 34, 54
Gilding 32-3, 46
Giza *9*, *9*, 28, 34
Gold 11, *13*, 14-16, 21, *22*, 32, 34, 41, 43, 57
Gold beater's skins 32, *33*
Gold leaf 32-3, *33*
Goldsmith *13*, 14, 20, 34, 38, 44-5, 60
Greece 56
Grinding 8, 13
Hammering 8, *9*, 28, 30, 35-6, *36*, 44, 47, 50-1, 53, 56
Hammer stones 28, 30-2, *33*, 36, *36*, *39*, 40
Hoes 56
Hooks 56
Horus 14, 17, *43*
India 19
Indonesia 19
Indus civilisation 19
Indus valley 7
Ingots *13*, 14-15, *19*, 19-21, 44
Inspector 59, 60
Iran *6*, 7-8, 19
Iron 11, 17-18, 20, 47, 53
Irrigation systems 7
Isis 14-15, *43*
Jewellers 14, 45, *45*, 46
Karnak 19, 25
Khaefre *10*, 34
Khartoum 18
Knives 54-7
Kom Ombo 55-6
Koptos 11
Kush 11
Lead 11, 14, 19, 20, 41
Leaded tin bronze 20-1, 25, 34
Levant *6*, 7
Limestone 17, 27
Lost wax casting 40, *41*, 41-2, *42*, *43*, 56
Maat 21
Malaysia 19
Mari 19
Meir 23, 28

Melting 8, 9, 14-15, 21-4, *25*, 27-8, 31, 41
Mercury 33
Merimda *6*, 8
Meroe 18
Mesopotamia *6*, 7-9, 17, 19
Meteoric iron 17
Miner 11, 13-14
Mining 7, *10*, 11-12, 14, 17, 20-1
Mitanni 17
Napata *10*, 11
Naqada *6*, 8, 16
Natron 34
Naucratis 17, 53
Needles 54-5
Nephthys 14
Nickel 11, 17
Nippur *6*, 7
Nomads 11
Nubia 11, 16, 18
Opening of the mouth 17, *18*
Ornamenting 46
Osiris 17
Overseer 12, *19*, 59-60
Peloponnese 17
Platinum 11
Polishing 8, 36-8, *39*, 41, 60
Prospecting 14
Ptah 60
Punt 16
Quban 14
Quseir el-Qadim 18, 20
Ramesses II 53
Ras Shamra 19
Razors 41, 56-7, *57*
Re 14, 21
Red Sea 11
Reducing 15
Refining 14, 17, 21, 28, 33
Repoussé work 46
Riveting 34, 41, 43
Roasting 15
Roman Empire 56
Salt 14, 34
Saqqara 22, 35, 37, *39*, 44
Saw 47, 50-1, 53, 56
Scissors 41, 55, 57
Semna *10*, 11
Seth 17
Seti I *25*, *26-9*, *38*
Settlement *6*, 7, 8
Shaft furnace 15, *16*
Shears 55-6
Shellal 17
Sickles 56
Silver 11, 15-17, 21, 32, 34, 41, 43
Sinai 14, 17, 23
Slag 15, 17

Smelting 8-9, 11, 14-15, *16*, 17-18, 20
Smelting furnace 9, 15, 60
Smiths 8, *9*, 20-1, 27-8, 30-1, 34, 36, *36*, 42, 46
Smoothing 28, 31, 36, *36*, 38, 50
Sobek *41*
Sokar *38*, 60
Soldering 34-5, 44, 46
Somalia 19
Spain 18
Spatulas 56
Steel 56
Sumerians 7, 8, 34, 40, 42
Syria 19-20
Tal i-Iblis *6*, 7
Tasa 8
Temple equipment 47
Tepe Asiab *6*, 7
Tepe Ganj Dareh *6*, 7
Tepe Hissar *6*, 7
Tepe Sialk *6*, 7
Thailand 19
Thebes *13*, 19, 24-5, *26*, *28-9*, 32, *39*, 40, 50, 52, 53-4
Tigris *6*, 8
Tigris-Euphrates valley *6*, 7-9
Timna 14
Tin 11, 14, 18-19, *19*, 20
Tin bronze 11, 19, 20-1, 34, 41-3, *43*, 47, 50, 53-7
Tongs 30, 35, 56
Tools 9, 14, 17, 20-1, 23, 28, 31-2, 36, 40, 46-7, *48*, 51, 53-6, 58
Trade 7-9, 11, 18, 19, 59-60
Tuyère 24, *24*, *25*, 27, 28
Tweezers 41, 56-8
Unas 37
Ur *6*, 7
Uruk *6*, 7
Wadi Abbed *10*, 11
Wadi Allaqi *10*, 11
Wadi Araba 14, 17
Wadi Dib 17
Wadi el-Fawakhir *10*, 11
Wadi el-Hudi *10*, 11, 13
Wadi Halfa 17
Wadi Hammamat *10*, 11
Wadi Marwat 17
Wadi Sid *10*, 11
Wawat 11
Weapons 9, 14, 20, 40, *48*, 56, 58
Weighing 21, *22*
Whitesmith 34-5, *36*, 60
Wire 42-6
Zagros Mountains *6*, 7-8
Zinc 11